THERE'S MORE TO CHURCH MUSIC THAN MEETS THE EAR

THERE'S MORE to CHURCH MUSIC THan MEETS THE EAR

Richard DeVinney

illustrated by Sandy Bauer

Fortress Press · Philadelphia

Library of Congress Catalog Card Number 72-75648

ISBN 0 - 8006 - 0118 - 1

Printed in the United States of America

3239E72   *1 - 118*

To all the delightful people
in the churches I have served
who have made this book possible
—and necessary

Contents

Preface

So you are a musician looking for a "church job." Let us assume, just for the sake of this book, that you are a competent but inexperienced organist and/or choir director and that you want to offer your talent to some unsuspecting church—or what is more likely, that you are a competent and experienced musician who occasionally has difficulty with some of the church people with whom you work. You are reading this book because you have found the church to be a mysterious body of persons of all shapes and kinds who seem to have one motive in common: to make life as miserable as possible for the musician.

In my years of firsthand observation (from the time my mother brought me home to the parsonage from the hospital) I have seen thoroughly capable musicians fired, not because they couldn't play the organ or direct the choir, but because they couldn't solve the mystery of dealing with that one element in the church without which most of us think the church would be perfect—the people.

The following collection of more or less random thoughts on the problem of public relations in the church's music department is an attempt to share some of the insights that I learned at my mother's knee and my father's desk, and thereafter as I toddled into the church alone fresh from six years of college lectures—not one of which prepared me to meet my first minister or music committee or choir.

In these days of confusion and uncertainty, when the very life of the church itself is said to be in danger and when the musician's place in it is being redefined, the need for us to understand church *people* as well as we do church *music* is greater than ever. Indeed, the very survival of the church musician as a species may depend on it.

Richard DeVinney

Letting Them Know They Want You

You have finally done it. Your graduation recital is over. You have your degree. You ask, "How do I get a job as a musician in the church?" Well, musicians have very little help. There are college placement offices. There are local councils of churches and the American Guild of Organists placement services. There are professional employment agencies, and there is luck. Most jobs are found by being in the right place at the right time—or having a friend who is. If you have none of these to start with, call the prominent church musicians in the area where you want to work. They will know where the openings are and will be happy to tell you of them unless they are planning to apply themselves.

Finding a job is usually not difficult. Getting it and keeping it are. This first chapter deals with the "getting." The "keeping" will take the rest of the book. Let us assume that you have found a church needing a person of your qualifications and you are about to apply. All you really have to do is let them know they want you.

The "Trials" in Getting Started

What should be your procedure in the interviews? If a church knows what it is doing it will subject you to some, if not all, of the following: a meeting with the minister, an interview with the music committee (at which time you will have to play for them if you are an organist), a rehearsal session with the choir (if you are a director), and a demonstration of your skills in an actual Sunday morning service.

As you approach these meetings consider these three basic principles: (1) When you perform for the committee it will be *what* you play, not *how* you play that will count. (2) When you direct the choir it will be *how* you direct, not *what* you direct that will count. (3) There will be two votes that matter. The first will be the minister's. You can get the job if he is noncommittal, but you cannot get it if he does not like you. The second vote will be the committee's. You can get the job if most of them like you, but you cannot get it if the high school band director or the church secretary (both of whom are on the committee) are not impressed. If you do not understand these simple principles you are truly a neophyte and you should read on.

Let us begin our discussion at the top. Now surely you know where the top is! Two out of every three of my jobs have been launched through a conversation with the minister's *wife*. When you first call the minister he will not be home. As you talk with his wife, be courteous and businesslike. Don't call his home on Saturday, Sunday afternoon, Monday, or at mealtime. These are the times he is most likely to be there—and least likely to want to talk to you. When you do reach him, be courteous and businesslike with him too. It is important that he and his wife agree in their first impression of you. If, when he hangs up, he says to her, "My, he was courteous and businesslike," and she replies, "That's what I thought too," you are practically hired.

Meeting the Minister

Your interview with the minister is critical. I have seen people hired for church staff positions on the word of the minister in spite of misgivings on the part of lay committees. I have also seen people dismissed from consideration by an otherwise favorably impressed committee after a wordless but knowing frown from the minister.

When you talk with him, assume the role of the professional who knows exactly what he is doing in the church. Don't talk about music. Even though he will discuss it as best he can, he will defer judgment on your musical skills to the musicians who will hear you. He will assume that you are skilled. What he wants to find out is how you will fit on his "team." In his questions he will be testing you in three categories: musical skills, how well you will work with him and other staff members and the congregation, and your requirements for salary, vacation, and fringe benefits.

Questions on musical skills will come first, but are least important now. Be brief in your answers and wait for the next set of questions. You will know he has arrived at this key category when he asks, "Why are you leaving your present position?" He probably already knows that you had a fist fight with the head usher, but he wants to see how you perform in a tight spot. As you discuss questions in this category, you must let him know in no uncertain terms what you think: that the church's total program is more important merely than its music program (if you don't think that, you should be looking into the job opportunities in plumbing or some other more lucrative field); that participation by people is at least as important as quality of performance; and that you think it important to call on people in their homes when you ask them to work in the church.

Let the entire interview remain in this key category if possible. He will be probing your views of the church and of work in it. This is your opportunity to probe his views too. You should not yet have decided finally whether you want this job, and the most important factor by far in your decision is the compatibility you envision between yourself and the minister. Ask him why he wants music in his church program. Ask him what he feels is the function of music in worship. Ask him some of the questions he is planning to ask you. This will do no harm, and he will be glad to note your interest and insight.

If you should get to questions concerning salary and other benefits give him a figure that you know is in line and let it go at that. Don't talk about vacation. I know a musician who lost a very good opportunity because his greatest concern during his initial interview was how much vacation he would be allowed. You should thoroughly discuss questions in this category before you accept the job, but not until after you make your favorable first impression.

A minister must satisfy himself that you are "safe." He wants to know that your personal life is above reproach, that you will not be abrasive with his people, and that you will be open to suggestions, if not directives, from him. Once he is assured of this, he will be so glad to find a musician of this kind that he will be on your side in the remainder of the meetings you must endure. We will come back to the minister in a later chapter. He really isn't such a difficult person to understand, and understand him you must—there is hardly a church around (looking for a musician) that can get along without him.

Meeting the Music Committee

Your second "trial" may very well be an interview with the music committee. This is as important as the meeting with the minister. The minister will be looking for reinforcement in his opinion of you. The committee will listen to him, and their vote will be decisive. You must make a favorable impression. Now that last sentence seemed obvious, didn't it? You must *make* an impression. This interview is where you take the *offensive*. You are there because you *want* the job. You are there to sell yourself. You must consciously give the committee as much insight as you can into your personality.

You should be enthused about music, the church, their church! You should show evidence of tact, humor, good judgment, serious purpose, organizational ability, maturity, emotional stability, aggressive salesmanship, cooperative spirit, musical skill, sound training, and "Christian character." These virtures are not listed here in order of importance. If they were, they would all have to be first.

How does one fill such an order? Just be yourself. Be at ease, at home with them. Don't try so hard to make an impression that you are absurd, but do talk. They want to know you. Each person will make up his mind about you by something you say—so keep talking.

Avoid debating matters of policy with them. Several of their most important questions will probably touch on points that have caused problems in the past. They will want to know how you feel about such things as the choir processing in step, or the children's choirs getting out of church school to rehearse, or the use of guitars in worship. Try to spot these "loaded" questions. If they concern relatively unimportant matters, be diplomatic in your answers. You can show that you have definite ideas on major issues. Save your strong opinions on minor inflammatory issues until you get the job and understand the people and the program. There might be good reasons for these things—or alternative ways of doing them—that you do not see right away.

Talk about experiences you have had. Don't brag, but tell about things you have done that were unique or outstanding. They want to hear some fresh ideas. Be inquisitive about the church. Ask questions about the people in the congregation that will show your interest. Ask about the amount budgeted for the music program (other than salary). If you don't ask about it, they will ask you what you think it should be. You cannot possibly answer intelligently without knowing what the budget figure covers, and what they have already in the way of library and equipment. If you ask this one first, you will learn more than they will. Show them bulletins and programs from your previous church—if you have had a previous church. The basic rule for this meeting is: keep talking.

They are looking for a pleasant personality, good training or good experience or both, and fresh ideas and enthusiasm. If you can produce two or three ideas that are new to them, a couple of statements reflecting sound opinions on the operation of a music program, and one or two good laughs for everyone, your interview will be a success. This interview is the point at which the major screening is done. It is absolutely crucial because you could lose out right here.

Showing What You Can Do at the Organ

If you are an organist and must play for the committee, you should give considerable care to the selection of the music you use. First of all, even though they do not request it, suggest that they hear you play a hymn. Choose a good, well-known

7

Call it a Postlude

hymn of praise and play it vigorously, as you would to accompany a congregation. With this simple beginning you can silence the most common complaint about organists: "He can really play recital pieces, but he can't play a simple hymn." The laymen does not know that hymn playing is not easy, and to be justified in his complaint he does not need to know.

Next play "your piece." Every organist has one piece that is spectacular. It was the first big piece you learned and you will never forget it—nor ever play anything else better. It is usually Bach's *Toccata and Fugue in D Minor* or Marcello's *Psalm 19*. Call it a postlude. Use the entire organ and show them you can handle it. But, don't stop there. Play something which you will call a typical prelude or offertory. This piece should be respectable (by a recognized composer) and have a melody. There are two kinds of people on music committees. You must satisfy them both with this piece. The musicians want to be assured that you like good music, and the nonmusicians want to be assured that you don't like good music too much. Fortunately, if you look carefully, you can find pieces that are good music and will still be liked by everybody.

Given the fact that you choose the right music and play it well, you shouldn't worry too much about this part of your interview. The organist-choir director gets his job on his work with the choir, and the part-time organist usually doesn't need an interview because there are many more part-time

organs than part-time organists. That leaves the
full-time organist, and he doesn't need to read this
book at all. All he needs to know besides how to
play the organ is that the director is in charge
even though he (the organist) is usually the better
musician. There is no other way.

Rehearsing the Choir

As a choir director you will probably be asked to
direct the choir for a portion of a rehearsal. No
part of your interview can help you more than making
a hit with the choir. This need not make you
nervous. You should welcome the opportunity to show
your skill in a situation in which you are in
command. You can control this session because it
involves the skills that you have learned best.
There is little excuse for this part of the "trial"
going any way but the way you want. There are,
however, some things to watch.

Choir members relish the experience of helping to
choose their own director. You should expect
several dynamics to begin operating the moment you
are introduced to them, and it is up to you to
neutralize the ones that can harm your cause and
exploit the ones that will be beneficial to it.
First, they will want to impress you. This is the
most natural feeling that a choir can have. Contrary
to what you might feel, they *will* try to sing
their best. They are proud of their choir, and they
will want you to like their singing. Second, they
will be critical of your every move. Each
individual wants to make his own choice to see if
the committee is right. They want to know what you

are like, what they might expect from you. This means that you will have their undivided attention. Third, unconsciously they still belong to their present (past) director. The way they have been singing is not only habitual with them; it is "right." These three things are important, and you can use them.

In the first place, the most potent force at work is probably their pride. They think they have a good choir. They want you to find this out. The best thing you can do is give them a compliment or two. Now, maybe they are not a very good choir. Maybe they have four sopranos, nine altos, seven tenors, and a baritone, or they have been without a director for six months, or their best nine singers are at a PTA meeting. One of the skills that all church musicians must have is the knack of finding something nice to say about people even if it requires special effort. Tell them how impressed you are with their pitch, or the way they watch you, or the way they pronounce "tree." Anything will do. Express pleasure with their work and they will respond with greater effort. Your attitude toward their singing will be reflected in their attitude toward you, and incidentally, in their singing.

Second, you will feel the very careful scrutiny of everybody in the room. Technically, the advantage in this is that they will be very responsive to your direction. But this kind of attention could bring tension to the rehearsal if you let it. You *must* rise above this danger. To dissipate the tension make them laugh. Humor will

Tell them how IMPRESSED you ARE with theIR PitcH

disarm people more quickly than anything else.
Strangely enough, humor breeds confidence. People
will give a person credit for talents and abilities
that he doesn't even have—if he can make them laugh.
In this very situation I once told a story that, had
my better judgment been in control, I would not have
used; but I told the story and I got the job. You
must break the ice. Humor is your tool.

Third, the fact that they are still inclined to
sing an anthem the way they always sang it in the
past should make you particularly alert to the way
they do the first few measures of each piece. Be
firm in what you do and demand from them what you
want, but be careful about what you change. An
extreme tempo, for instance (especially one a great
deal slower than the one to which they are
accustomed), will depress a choir more quickly than
anything else. The fact that you disagree with their
last director is irrelevant. It is important that
you show them something in the music that they
haven't discovered before, but make it in the area
of diction or dynamics or in the meaning of the
text—anything less controversial than tempo. Don't
change their entire concept of the piece either. It
is too risky.

Demonstrating on Sunday

We come now to a "trial" which is wholly
dependent on musical skill. We shall avoid
discussing musical skills at every turn since books
like that already abound. However, we said in the
beginning of this chapter that you might be asked to

demonstrate your ability in an actual service. Well, once the prelude begins, your captivating personality, which got you this far with these people, can no longer help you. You are now entirely at the mercy of your training and experience. But, if our premise is valid, you already have the job. This service is just their insurance. They probably wouldn't ask you to come on a Sunday morning if they were not pretty well settled in their decision.

The interviews, then, just like the work itself in the church, depend on your ability to handle yourself with people. It is really simple to get a job in the church. You just have to work at letting them know they want you.

Coming and Going

Do you know whether you are coming or going? You should know at all times. Obviously, how long you stay in a given position depends on many things, but normally your work will have a definite life-span. You will bring new ideas to the program each year, but you may eventually run out of things to try in each situation. Your program will reach a peak in its growth and from then on, unless your capacities grow faster than your program, your work will begin to wane. The sensitive director of any program knows this and will watch for it as an indicator that the time has come to look for a new position. The trick, of course, is to realize before anyone else does that you are on your way out, and then actually to leave while it is still *your* choice.

This chapter is about your first weeks on the job, and your last. There are unique opportunities available to you both when you are coming and when you are going. After examining these, we will deal in the remainder of the book with the very difficult years (or months) between.

Coming

Your biggest help on coming to a new position in the church is the "honeymoon." This is no imaginary interval of time; it is real, and easily measured. It begins when you arrive and ends the day a significant number of people come to a firm opinion about you and your work. The people will be curious and will give you their undivided attention for at least a month or two. They have been told by the minister that you are just the person they have been seeking. You should use this time for more than just trying to prove him right or wrong.

Unlike the first week of a marriage where little is accomplished in terms of building the relationship, this can be a fruitful time for the wise church worker. Until it is over, you will have *no* problems with people because nobody knows for sure yet whether or not you do things the way they think you should. Only when they figure that out will you start having problems—and then the "honeymoon" is over. But during this crucial time you can do two things that will be of immeasurable help to you for as long as you serve that congregation.

Making the "Honeymoon" Count

The first is this. Remembering (if you are a choir director) that for you the most important group of people in the church is the adult choir, tell the choir members that in the first six weeks you want to meet with them individually in their homes. Hang on—I'm as timid as you are about calling in people's homes (the books always recommend it, and I always send out letters). But this is different. Set up a schedule of times when you can come, and let your choir people sign up as an invitation for your call. Even if you are shy you will feel all right about going—because you were invited! Schedule two calls—no more—in one evening. Try to allow an hour and a half for each. Give your full attention to getting to know your people and their ideas one at a time.

The beauty of this plan is evident. You get acquainted fast, and this is important. Your people are immediately more loyal to you if they feel that you understand them. Then too, you get to hear all their suggestions and complaints. Most people have at least one thing that they would like to see done or not done, and they will tell you about it more readily now than at any other time. You can listen without committing yourself because you are new. Take notes after you get back in the car. When you have called on everyone, you can read to the choir a list of the often conflicting suggestions and gently kid them into realizing how many sides there are to most issues.

You will find that this first call in the home, where you meet the family and see each choir member in his own environment, will build the foundation for a growing relationship with singers as persons. After seven years in one church I still remember vividly many of the calls I made, and they have provided a basis for conversations and relationships with individuals ever since. The choir director who knows his singers well will never lack response from his choir.

You can also use the "honeymoon"—before it ends all too soon—to study the entire congregation. As you meet people you will begin to find the centers of influence. Look for strong people—not just vocal people but strong people. Look for the competent musicians who do not say very much, but whose opinion is heard. There are financial stalwarts who will give you tangible help if they feel your program deserves it. There are the active people who are the workhorses of the church and can be found wherever time and talent are needed. When you spot these people it is only common sense that you will seek their approval and support. Since you are new, ask their advice. Later on you may not feel that you want to do this, but right now you can get them to talk to you about their church and to share their enthusiasm for it. Try everywhere to build relationships of trust, mutual respect, and genuine friendship based on common interests. These relationships will be of great worth to you and your work in the years to come.

Perhaps right now is the time for me to deal with some feelings you may be having about this book—that it occasionally smacks more of advice for the politician than for the dedicated servant of Jesus Christ. I have worried about this from the beginning, wondering whether my suggestions for "dealing" with people would be construed by some readers to mean that people are to be manipulated or used. Nothing could be further from my intentions. Be patient. In a later chapter I will try to lay aside all doubts about proper motives and methods for the church musician. For now, just remember our premise that far too few musicians have the good sense to recognize that they are working with *people* as well as *music*. The principles of group dynamics, personal motivation, program building, and salesmanship must be understood by the church musician because people (unfortunately or fortunately—you choose) are people, in the church and out.

For Early Attention

We should consider three more things about your "coming." They deserve your attention in the days and weeks immediately ahead. First of all, if you have a sense of humor and can use it naturally on occasions when you are introduced to groups in the church, you have a powerful tool for gaining congregational support. Full-time musicians especially are expected to enter into the life of the church, to report to the governing bodies, and to serve on committees. If you can show nothing more than a sense of humor on your first greetings to these groups, you will have made friends where you will need them.

Second, be deliberate in your planning for change. I once worked with a minister who had a very workable, if cautious, method for beginning his work at a new church. The first year he spent getting acquainted with the program of the church as it was. The second year he began thinking of changes. The third year he made changes in the program as he saw them to be appropriate.

Obviously, this three-year plan would not be too dynamic an approach if you were only going to be

... make some kind of peace
with your PREDECESSOR

around for two years, but the principle is sound. If you begin with the proposition that there is a reason for the way they have always done things, you will try to discover that reason before you make the change. Hurried changes often result in a return to the old way eventually—much to the embarrassment of the director.

People will allow you a given amount of change, depending on such factors as their openness, your diplomacy and persuasive powers, and their respect for your judgment. Guard this reserve of readiness on their part. Never let it get depleted. Then when something comes along that is very important to you, they will allow you to make the change with very little complaint.

Finally, when you come into a new position you always must make some kind of peace with your predecessor. If he was extremely popular and left happily, your problem is that of "filling his shoes." If, however, it appears that he was extremely unpopular and left unhappily, you had better assure yourself, before you accept the position, that the rift was actually his fault. Unfortunately, even in churches there are "situations" in which no person can be successful. But, if your predecessor was genuinely bad, you might find it relatively easy to follow him. Here, then, is another principle to observe: if your predecessor was there for a long time, the people will probably be less disposed to make changes than if they are used to having leadership changes more or less regularly.

The predecessor that will give the most difficulty is the one who will not let go. This is the one who corresponds regularly with half of the choir, comes back to visit often, and invites your people to come and see him. We will say more about this under the rubric "going." In any event, your predecessor put the stamp of his personality on the program and you must deal with it. Generally speaking you should be wary of carrying on an argument with him by criticizing the program he has left behind. Praise him when you can: it will cost you nothing and will help you with his friends. The important principle to remember is that a congregation that can love one minister or musician has the capacity to love another also. The ideal predecessor to have (or be) is the capable, popular, well-loved musician who, when he leaves, moves at least five states away.

Going

Besides suggesting that you put distance (physical or otherwise) between yourself and your former church, I want to point out some other ways to be a successful predecessor. Common courtesy is motive enough for wanting to do this. Following a poor predecessor affords added incentive.

When you decide to leave a church and have gone through the delicate timing and negotiations sometimes involved in securing a new position, take some care in your departure. First of all, be neat. Leave files, enrollment lists, library, and office in good order. If you have begun a filing project in the music library, complete it. If membership lists, addresses, and telephone numbers are out of date, bring them up to date. You can do this in a fraction of the time it would require for someone new who does not know the people involved. Leave copies of old programs and bulletins; they are priceless reading for your successor.

Tell people, especially the youth who don't know how they will live without you, that you want them to stick by the choir. It is probable that they will be as fiercely loyal to the next director as they were to you.

If possible, schedule your leaving at a convenient time (like July), give the church as much notice as possible, then leave. And don't go back. Any friendships which you maintain should be maintained discreetly. Remember, somebody else is trying to deal with your ghost. Don't haunt him any more than you have to.

Church musicians often talk about the "professional" aspects of their positions. They want their profession to command respect in the sense that law and medicine do. We should merit that respect by practicing an ethical code as sophisticated as that of the other professions. One of the basic tenets of this unwritten code for church workers is that when the moving van comes the people belong to someone else. You must now find new friends in a new church.

The MAN UpStairs

The first relationship which a church musician should examine, evaluate, and develop is his relationship with the senior minister. There is no more crucial relationship for any staff member in a church. You *must* get along with him. Either he will help you or he will make your work impossible. You will find his position so important to everything that you do that he should be your main concern when you consider taking a position. I have known only one musician who has won a battle with his minister—and he decided it wasn't worth it. The minister is the administrative head of the church. His position has a symbolic significance that goes far beyond his purely legal status in relation to the staff. There is a sense in which the congregation feels that he *is* the church. If you attack him, you attack the church. The church will suffer and so will you.

In his dealings with you, the minister's foremost tool is an intelligence system that rivals that of the CIA. He knows almost everything that is happening in his church. On Monday morning, from 9:00 until 11:30, his telephone rings steadily with calls from church members who feel it necessary to report, inform, praise, suggest, and complain (not usually in that order). Our harried clergyman is thus aware of nearly everything that happens, is going to happen, or had better happen throughout his congregation. This gives him an immediate and decisive advantage over you.

Remembering Who's in Charge

Whether you think it right or not, it is the minister who is in charge. Regardless of how you assess his judgment or ability as an administrator, the administrative functions of a church will reflect that judgment and ability. No amount of pushing, pulling, persuading, or fighting on your part will change the course of the entire organization. The health and stability of a congregation will rise and fall on the leadership he provides. Indeed, it is my observation that a church, after several years, assumes the very personality of its minister. I have seen stable, personable, mature ministers turn a church into a stable, friendly congregation. And I have seen neurotic, disorganized, insecure ministers actually transfer these characteristics to a local congregation (not individuals) as a whole. I have sensed this same transfer taking place with respect to the minister's personal emphases and interests, whether or not he consciously tries to impose them on the group. I will leave it for the reader to make his own analysis of specific situations, but a sensitive observer with broad experience could document this principle many times.

All this is to say that a staff member of a church must accept the fact that his fortunes are inevitably tied to those of his minister. A mature, experienced musician *can* have a successful time in a church with almost any minister; but if the minister has important faults, the musician, to succeed, must have some of the qualities the minister lacks—and even then he probably will not enjoy his position or stay with it very long. A much more common pattern is for a musician to find fault with his boss, then discover that his boss is finding fault with him. Communication is thus broken off and the *musician* soon leaves.

Let us examine the broad area between congenial and creative teamwork, on the one hand, and irrevocable breakdown of all relationship between minister and musician, on the other. We shall look for ways to work *with* and *for* what we shall call the "difficult" minister.

This portion of our discussion is approached with apprehension, since ministers, because of their position, enjoy a certain immunity from public criticism. This immunity is only a public one, however, as any parishioner will admit who savors "roast preacher" around the Sunday dinner table. I am certain that no single topic is more on the minds of musicians. Their conversations at mealtimes, their informal discussions at institutes and conferences are filled with one common problem: the clergy. Ministers are analyzed, discussed, berated, dissected, and bemoaned—nobody seems to know what to do about them. We give each other advice about every other problem that comes up, but when someone says, "My minister doesn't even like the *Messiah*," we all shake our heads and give a large dose of sympathy without applying any of the ingenuity with which we tackle the problems of poor organs, lack of tenors, or third-grade monotones.

I am not saying that all or even most ministers are guilty of causing problems. I am suggesting that the *relationship* between minister and musician is more often than not less helpful than it might be: minister doesn't understand musician because of his "artistic" peculiarities and his technical skill, musician doesn't understand minister because rare is the minister who lives up to the image that we all project for him. I am going to get around eventually to suggesting that ministers are "only" people and deserve our charity; and later on I will even suggest that musicians are sometimes the cause of their problems themselves. For now, let us see if we can isolate some common faults of the clergy. Once the ministers are unmasked we can accept them for the human beings that they are and look for ways we can work with them.

Getting Along with "Difficult" Ministers

Taking a cue from students of group dynamics let us identifiy some "roles" which ministers often play. Group psychologists like to talk about "dominators," "gatekeepers," and "icebreakers." These are names given to people as they play various roles in a group experience. I would like to describe some ministerial roles in the relationship between minister and musician. Keep in mind that one minister can play several roles at different times. These roles will be found in various degrees in all people, and rarely in the degree to be described here. Our pictures are obviously caricatures, drawn boldly and without care for detail. They are all negative, so do not look for them in living people you know—if they are not really there. Remember that the faults we see first in others are often the faults we have ourselves. So be charitable; these "ministers" could be musicians! If you start feeling triumphant because I have described your minister, turn to the next to last chapter—you may find yourself.

"How Big Was the Crowd?"

You work hard for eight weeks—planning, choosing music, rehearsing choirs, publicizing, practicing, arranging for ushers and programs, lining up singers, calling parents, and sweating out colds, sore throats, and pneumonia. The big night comes. You haven't slept for days. You go through your carefully detailed plans. The choirs sing better than they know how. Everybody is thrilled. You walk breathlessly up to your minister and he says, "How big was the crowd?"

About the only tangible measure of success for a program is the count of people or money, or both. If "success" has to be affirmed every time there is a program in the church, obviously the size of the crowd is going to be important. But, when that is the only concern, or even the primary concern, there is a great danger that a person will grow less and less sensitive to the actual value of the program itself.

This minister will want the children's choirs to sing for church dinners and evening mission programs, not admitting that people have long since caught on to this not-so-subtle method of getting parents to attend. Don't fight him with preachments on the purpose of children's choirs. His insecurity about the total program is too strong. His problem is basic. You should constantly point out to him the quality in the church's program and help him to feel the rewards of doing things well in spite of the attendance.

Success is the basic answer for this problem. Have a successful program and the crowd will be big. When the minister feels that the church is successful he will become more secure and will spend less time standing in the back counting heads and more time actually listening to the program or participating in it.

"You'd Better Do It _This_ Way"

You need new choir robes. Your music committee meets and develops a plan to raise the money. They choose a color and style. You help them organize to undertake the project and then you go to see the minister. He listens as you tell him your plans and then he says, "Your idea is all right, but you'd better do it _this_ way."

This minister is the interferer. He is a tough one. He has been in the ministry for thirty years and has seen all kinds of musicians come and go. He always

You'd better Do it This Way

knows what should be done and how to do it. New
ideas are never new to him. Everything fits into
his established perspective and if your idea hasn't
already been tried in his present church it has in
one of his former ones. He expects the church will
always be the same—and his probably will! There is
a right way and a wrong way to do almost everything.
The first is his way and the second is yours.

He is of the old school, achieved his present
position by seniority, and will doubtless retire
from the church. He runs a smooth program and
equates this tranquillity with success.

Your problem with him comes not from his inertia,
but from his directives to you. His ideas about
music in worship are out of date. He orders you to

play softly during all prayers, sing a favorite but terrible gospel hymn as a "theme song" every Sunday during Lent, and have the choir process in step with square corners on the outside foot.

But take heart. Although this man is probably the most difficult to work with, he is not impossible. He has a fatal weakness. He is so confident of his program and he has been around for so long that he is almost certainly not a planner. Your greatest tool for working with him is the well-laid plan. Be certain that you have your program and your programs planned thoroughly, and the scheduled dates selected and approved well ahead. Get the important musical occasions on the church calendar early. Then the last-minute requests will have to fit around your carefully planned and rehearsed program. Go to the minister with ideas and plans six months ahead if they need his approval. The issues will be practically academic from that distance and will be ruled on with objectivity. Then when he comes to you on Tuesday and wants you to get the choir to a massed choir presentation next Sunday afternoon with rehearsals Wednesday, Thursday, and Friday nights you can remind him that last summer he gave you permission to have a choir picnic on that day and it is too late now to change.

"Let's Have Some Special Music"

The longest business meeting of the year is next Wednesday night. It is an all-church meeting and reports must be given for the year by each auxiliary organization; the budget must also be approved and the calendar planned for the coming year. You happen to meet the minister on the street and he says, "Next Wednesday night is a pretty important meeting for the church. Let's have some special music right after the devotions."

It seems to you that the most important verse in the Bible for this minister is: "Whenever two or three are gathered together, we should have special music." The minister is neither easy to understand nor to satisfy. His idea of an effective program is based on quantity and variety. He thinks that a long, dull meeting is made more attractive by having some "entertainment" which has a "message." You will have to leave the problem of the long, dull meeting to the leaders of the church to solve, but you have every right to frown on the idea of adding length (and sometimes dullness) to the meeting with music that is often arranged in desperate haste (remember the meeting is *next* Wednesday).

One problem is that when he sees you frown he interprets it as laziness or lack of cooperation on your part, just because he has asked you to do some extra work. Your answer to this one is not simple. Your only hope is to try to make him understand that you sincerely do not believe in using sacred music as entertainment, and that even though you are a musician you think that there are some times—this may be one—when people would rather get their business done and get home than hear someone sing.

"_ _ _ _ _ _ _ _ _"

You are like every other church musician. You have good Sundays and you have bad ones. Some days the choir sings like angels and the organ playing is inspired. Other days the choir sounds unrehearsed and the organ seems to manufacture its own wrong notes. But, no matter what the results, whenever you are able to get the minister to notice that you are around, his comment about the music program is "_ _ _ _ _ _ _ _ _ _ _ _."

This minister appears intentionally to ignore music and musicians except when it is "necessary" publicly to acknowledge your work. He does not seem to think that music is important to anyone. After all, he himself is totally wrapped up in the preaching, administration, and pastoral care that make up his ministry. Indifference is usually uncomfortable for anyone to accept, and sometimes difficult to work beside. The church musician is no exception. However, the minister who appears not to care about the music program, or even be aware of it, is probably not what he seems.

It is inconceivable that any minister could be totally insensitive to the importance of music for many people in his congregation. Probably, what you interpret as indifference is really something else. The minister may be a person who is completely consumed by his own work and never allows his thoughts to range much beyond it. He may be a thoroughly nonmusical person who does not understand the amount of work required to make music, or who does not respond even to the best when he hears it. Or, he may actually be paying you a compliment by leaving the direction of the program up to you. He may be deliberately trying to avoid interfering with you, and you may be interpreting this as his ignoring you. It is even remotely possible that the music you produce *deserves* to be ignored.

Whatever the case, the receiver of the "signal" of indifference usually exaggerates what he senses. To be ignored is hard to accept. It also requires you to develop independence. So, cheer up. Make your own decisions, he won't care. Indeed, he is the easiest "difficult" minister to work with because under him you are pretty much free to do as you please.

You can help him to be aware of the music program if you keep him informed. Put in his mailbox a copy of all correspondence to choir members, all programs in which you are involved, minutes of all committee meetings, and regular reports of all kinds. He will then be aware of what you are doing, even if only as these papers travel to the waste basket.

He probably cares more than you realize. Keep trying. Even if he does not notice your music he will appreciate your ministry.

"Just Don't Cut into the Sermon Time"

In your summer planning you come across a *Te Deum* by a contemporary composer that you really like. It is just what the choir needs as a challenge. Eight and one-half minutes long, it will take a lot of work to prepare. You go in to see the minister to ask him about doing an anthem that long some Sunday and he says, "Sure it's all right, but just don't cut into the sermon time."

The "Big Ego" is the minister that causes problems for all other church staff members. He is usually thirty-five to forty-five years of age, has his Phi

Just don't cut into the SERMON TIME

Beta Kappa key from a distant school, has served on one of the denominational boards, and has written two short devotional books and several magazine articles. His main interest is "theology"—which means preaching. He is an excellent preacher but dislikes music (because he must listen to it—it won't listen to him).

Usually, this minister wants you to "succeed," that is, make a splash with your program. But he does not want you to make a *personal* splash. It is your *program* that must succeed. He wants everything in "his" church to be the best. You will have conflict with him only when you threaten him personally by becoming too popular or when your music threatens to take over some of the "sacred" thirty minutes of sermon time.

I don't think that it is improper to admit that there are ministers like this. (Musicians with big egos are even more numerous.) Indeed, a big ego is almost a necessary part of the really "successful" person's equipment. There are few outstanding preachers or outstanding anything elses who do not have a highly developed ego. This is what provides the drive for them to work hard. But, the preacher who is also a pastor must have his ego under control. Therein lies maturity.

Of all the difficult ministers, the "Big Ego" is the one that the full-time musician will encounter most often. This is because full-time musicians are in large churches, and the "Big Ego" nearly always succeeds in becoming the pastor of a large church. It is also true, however, that the days of the "pulpiteer" who can do little else but preach are fading fast.

Suppose you find yourself in the shadow of a pulpit performer, whether in a large church or a small one. First of all, don't threaten him. Never play your popularity against his. You must support him because, as we said earlier, he *is* the church. Be concerned about the church's total program. Do not take part in any complaining you may hear among the lay people. Grouchy gossip could make you feel better, but it can also lead to no good. Show that you are secure enough to work without sharing the "glory" and the minister will let you alone.

The bonus that you sometimes get with the "Big Ego" is independence. He may not want to take the time to bother you at all. If so, count this a plus and ignore the rest.

"Can You Play Softly Just before the Cymbal Crash?"

This minister has a flare for the dramatic. He believes worship is a drama and that the way to combat boredom and lethargy in the congregation is to shock, thrill, mystify, frighten, or entertain those who come. He prides himself on his own "creativity" and will dream up ideas that *will* shock and mystify you. As he excitedly describes the impact that his latest creation is going to make

on the people he asks, "Can you play softly for ten seconds just before the cymbal crash?"

You will inevitably have to play the role of the conservative with this minister. He is not easy to work with because he has no real understanding of worship itself. A moving service of worship must indeed have a powerful dramatic aspect, but real drama is usually more subtle than he can appreciate.

You can probably put limits on his wild ideas by pleading your lack of skill at improvisation or your ignorance about just what kind of music can best depict such awesome things as earthquakes and storms. You will just have to accept your resultant "wet-blanket" role and counter with carefully thought-out ideas about worship. Grit your teeth, close your eyes when the lights flash, plug your ears when the cymbal crashes, and hope one day seminaries will include some healthy courses in the meaning and purpose of worship.

I could go on and on with more examples of the "difficult" minister, but I have already been far more unkind to our colleagues than I really feel I should. I think it is safe to say that being a minister is not only one of the most difficult jobs in the world, but it is getting worse, and fast. Every person in the church has come to be an authority on what a minister should be like. The minister's only escape is to hide in his theology books just as we hide in our practice rooms. Wise are the churches—and the church musicians—who accept their minister for what he is, and who accept what he can offer, faults and all.

Almost every problem that musicians have with their ministers is caused by a lack of communication. If you can achieve a reasonable level of openness with your "boss" and talk freely even about the things that bother you in each other, your problems will be kept small in number and relatively unimportant. Then you can direct your energies to the significant work that calls you both.

Cease-fire on the Battleground

If the minister is the most important individual for the church musician to understand, the adult choir is by far the most important group. The reputation of the church choir as a battleground may or may not be deserved. The choir's difficulties probably get attention only because it is the most visible group in the church. It must present itself to the public each week, and each month must meet more often than any other group. At the same time it is a diverse group bringing together people of many ages and kinds because of a common interest (music) that by itself has a curious inability to solve personality conflicts.

It seems strange that the concert choir in school or college can be so closely bound together by its singing while the church choir almost never benefits from the musical bond of unity. This is probably due to the fact that the church choir rarely achieves the polished singing of a memorized concert. Sunday anthems and seasonal cantatas are sung in various stages of repair with varying personnel in the choir loft. The exultant satisfaction of a flawless, memorized performance is rare in the church.

The problem for the director, then, is to lead this diverse group to a feeling of oneness, using music if possible, but certainly using patience, tact, humor, and enthusiasm. Unity of spirit is sought not only because the choir will sound better and problems will be fewer, but because group unity is an ingredient of the Christian community which should be the goal for all endeavors in the church.

Getting Acquainted with the Choir

The first project you should undertake with your choir is to get acquainted. We have talked already about calling on the members during your "honeymoon." This is the beginning. But you must also keep in mind at all times that these choir members are people—individual persons whom you are meeting twice a week. It is too easy to think of them merely as singers: good singers, bad singers, leaders, followers, tenors, or altos. It is too easy to think of them simply as choir members: dependable, late, eager, complainers, or helpers. It is too easy to think of them as a group. But, if they are going to rally around you as their leader each must feel that he knows you in some special way. You are not going to like them all. Few of them will be the kind of person you would specifically seek out for companionship in a crowded room, but it is possible to have some interest or experience in common with each. Your first encounter (remember the call in their home?)

provides the tiny seed of your relationship. It must be nurtured carefully. Every chance you get you must build on this common interest. You will find that what might have started out as a somewhat selfish effort to win a supportive choir member will soon turn into a two-way relationship that will find both of you giving and receiving benefits.

All this sounds rosy and idealistic, and it is. No one is capable of deep personal relationships with twenty or thirty different people. There will be people who will defy your ability to break through (we'll discuss them later), but always have in mind that these are *persons* whom you are serving. They are not just parts of a musical instrument.

As you get acquainted you must also consider your relationship to the group. Much has been written in the "how to" books about this: you should start rehearsals on time and end them on time; you should plan ahead carefully and know exactly what you want to do at every moment; you should make changes gradually and perform their favorite anthems occasionally and choose a wide variety of music so that you will not be accused of being in a rut; you should keep them informed about your plans for them. All of these things are important. But there are other equally important things that are sometimes forgotten or ignored.

Allow them to know you. Be sure you don't have a "choir rehearsal" personality that acts like a shield to keep them from knowing what you are really like. There is nothing more deadening than the musician who is so intense about his music and his work that he cannot allow a little fun in the rehearsal. And the best kind of fun is at his own expense.

We musicians have a common quality. We all take ourselves too seriously. For example, no one will deny that a choir should look uniform if it is visible during the service; this is why choirs wear robes. But really, is the history of church music in the twentieth century going to be greatly changed if an alto wears blue shoes instead of black some Sunday morning? Care about details, of course, but be fussy only about important things.

Open up to the choir. Let them know the aspects of your personality that have nothing to do with music. They will join the choir, stay with it, and cooperate readily only if they respect you as a person too.

Working with Individuals

Partly because musicians, like all artists, are inherently more sensitive, and partly because the act of singing requires a person to expose a portion of himself for approval, it is almost inevitable that there will be conflicts of personality in a volunteer choir. Let us draw some more caricatures and see if there are suggestions to be made for working with what we will call "those difficult people in the choir."

Talented Prima Donna

Our first "difficult" singer is not found in every choir, but when he is, he is immediately recognizable. It is absolutely necessary that you establish your relationship with him at once. He has the best voice in the choir and will admit it freely. The problem is that he does not work at it. He gets by on solo repertoire that he has known for years. He treats the irregularities in his voice as symptoms of various illnesses—and he is almost never completely healthy. He will not accept any correction even when he makes mistakes, but will not hesitate to correct the director or the accompanist, especially in front of the choir.

In order to be his choir director you must assert yourself. Be better prepared than he is. Know the music better than he does. Don't make a point of it, just be sure of yourself and don't make mistakes. Remember, he doesn't work at it. It is not too difficult to stay ahead of him. Challenge him. Give him a solo that will require him to work. Let him know that other singers you have worked with have been able to sing it, and offer to work with him. He must gain respect for your musicianship. When he does, he will do his best for you.

Untalented Prima Donna

This person is usually in her forties and unhappy about that. Her position as section leader has been either eliminated or taken from her and she is unhappy about that. Fewer and fewer people each year can remember when she was the only soloist in the choir and she is unhappy about that. Her problem is not so much that her voice is deteriorating— although it may be—but that she never did have a very good one. Her real problem is that the growth

and improvement of the choir, and the increasing sophistication of the listeners, have made her position in the choir less secure.

Her great need is to be told again and again how dependent you as the director are on her help in the choir. She has a predictable way of asserting herself, of getting attention, and of threatening you when she is upset. This all-purpose weapon is "the quit." It will happen like this: on Sunday afternoon you will get a telephone call from someone else—never directly from her—that she has quit the choir. The proper way to handle this kind of quit is to ignore it—if you are sure you can distinguish this attention-seeking quit from the real one. It never lasts more than two weeks. It will get less and less frequent if you never mention it when she comes back.

You can help this person. She is extremely insecure and needs acceptance from someone. Give her that acceptance at times when she is not causing problems, and the problem times will become fewer. Tell her you need her. You do. Give her occasional solos that she can handle. Keep her busy. Ask her questions about the past experiences of the choir. Make her feel that she is helpful. She desperately needs her choir membership. You are her "minister" and can perform a significant role in helping her gain the security she must have.

Guardian of the "Old School"

This is usually a tenor. He has been in the choir for thirty years or more. He has even directed the choir on occasion and yearns for the good old days.

He likes ten-minute, eight-part, Victorian anthems and thinks you should choose them regularly even though the first sopranos may have to hold high "A" for measures at a time and none of yours has more than a passing acquaintance with a high "G." He remembers very well the days when the choir had great voices and great directors, and he loses no opportunity to tell you about both.

There is an experiment you can try with this person that might prove very instructive. Choose carefully an anthem that is not among the best of the old "war-horses." Make sure it is one he knows well—some old bulletins or programs will tell you this. If you look long enough you will find an anthem that is long and repetitive and full of the dotted rhythms and dramatic clichés that characterized his golden age. Get the music out some night in rehearsal and don't say a word. There is every possibility that the younger members of the choir will react strongly and vocally against the anthem and your tenor will hear—from someone other than yourself—that times have changed.

The Adviser

This is usually a woman. She is a schoolteacher. She is not married. She teaches either grade school or high school English. You are her "student" and you need her help. During rehearsals she will regularly and often give you suggestions, reminders, corrections, the results of her polls, and lessons in grammar. For her, the most important thing about the choir's breathing is not how, but when, and if you are able to get all the phrases in the right place it doesn't really matter what the singing itself sounds like.

You must understand this person. She does not think she is more capable than you. She does not want to "run things." Her pattern of making suggestions and giving advice is compulsive. Your only way of handling her successfully is to have patience and more patience. In rehearsal, keep things moving. Always know what you want and what you are going to do next. Never allow that little moment of uncertainty to arise. Don't ask the choir for opinions. And once a year, quietly but firmly, remind her that, for better or worse, you are the director.

The Griper

This person is a paradox. He is almost always someone who is enthusiastic about music and especially about singing. But, for some reason, he will punctuate most rehearsals with complaints. Sometimes he talks out loud so that the entire choir can hear him. More often he mutters so that only his section can hear. He probably doesn't like the music selected for next Sunday. And he certainly disagrees with your interpretation of the anthem you like and he does not.

I guess it is not surprising after all that he really likes to sing. He would have to be especially enthusiastic about music to stay in a choir that makes him so miserable. The griper is definitely a negative influence on the morale of the choir, but you must never allow his complaining to affect you. His problem has nothing to do with you or the disagreements among them. You will also learn from choir's work. If it did, you would not hear his complaints. People who have real complaints about leadership, at least in the church, almost never voice them in the group. They tell their friends in private how they feel. This person's problem is one he has at home, or in his work, or in his personal life. He is an unhappy person.

You can do two things with him. First, you can be his friend. He probably is not even aware of his constant complaining, much less of his real problem. Cultivate a friendly relationship with him and he will become more conscious of the problem he is causing you. The basic problem, though, is really his, not yours. And second, ignore his gripes in rehearsal. Never acknowledge them and they won't bother the choir so much. Your strategy for this person is: never allow him to sit next to a new person in the choir.

Not every member of the choir is going to be thrilled with you or your work. Some may not even like you. There will be people who react negatively because they liked your predecessor, or because they would themselves like to direct the choir, or simply because they are negative people. Usually, what you sense as hostility toward you is actually a problem *within them* that has nothing to do with you or the choir. As you try your best to be sensitive to your choir members as individuals you will develop a relationship with each one that will allow you to know his true feelings. This will make it easier for you to reconcile differences and them, thereby improving your skill in relating to other persons, in this case singers. You must study and practice this skill just as surely as you do your musical skills if you are to effect not only a limited truce on the "battleground," but true harmony in the choir.

Leaving a Good Taste in their Ears

We have acknowledged earlier that the greatest anxiety a church musician feels is usually at the point of his relationship to his minister. Perhaps his next most common concern has to do with his frustrations about the low musical taste of the people in his congregation and even in his choir. To the degree that he feels this frustration at all, it is with him continually. One of the greatest demands on his time is the never-ending task of choosing music for each Sunday, for each special program, for each choir, and for each instrument. Whenever he looks at a piece of music he must judge its acceptability. Too often he feels shackled in his choice by the apparent lack of musical understanding and appreciation that his people express.

What Is Sacred Music?

Before we tackle the practical aspects of this problem we should step back a little and talk about the need for good music in the church. Usually the church musician gets very dogmatic at this point and intones one of his most cherished dogmas: "God deserves our best (music)," or "Only our best (music) is worthy of being offered to God."

Now there is nothing wrong with these pious statements. They are perfectly defensible and should in some way be a part of the church musician's understanding of his task. But their impact, when used to defend a good piece or attack a bad one, is likely to be no more effective than any other dogmatic or pious phrase in the church today. The problem is: after you have said all this and the sound has died away, what do you say, or do, next? Can you expand on the idea? Can you clarify and undergird it? Can you define your point by broadening its impact rather than by just repeating yourself in ever more dogmatic and pious terms?

How do you respond, for instance, when a person says to you, " 'Jesus Loves Me This I Know' is the very best music that I know how to offer to God"? Do you then make a judgment about that person? If you are going to use a theological argument as a justification for good music in the church (and you should), then you had better back up that argument with an adequate understanding of the theology itself.

Paul Tillich, recently deceased theologian, left an insight for which artists and musicians will always be grateful. Tillich did not look up in the sky for God, he found him in the very depths of life's experiences. For Tillich it was necessary to get beneath the superficial and the obvious, and to feel, sense, and hear God in the profound experiences and thoughts of each of us each day. The theologian thus implied that man's search for God should take him to levels of meaning that can best be reached by the poet, the artist, and the musician. Music that has depth of meaning will be the most helpful to the worshiping Christian.

Try talking less about "good" music and "bad" music and talk more about profound, rich, powerful, dynamic, intense music and pale, trite, banal, obvious, weak, tired music. Talk about what music can offer that goes beyond a tickling of the eardrums or a tug at the memory. With Tillich, we can say that music which touches the depths of the meaning of the gospel will be the most valid for use in worship.

Having said this, it is *not* your job to take the matter one step further and make good music an end in itself. Music is not the most important thing in the church. We work hard to produce good music because it is the most effective kind for *church use.* It is not to be music for the sake of music, but music for the sake of the worshiper in the pew. Our "dogma" is then a much more understandable and acceptable one: we can express our praise more adequately and be moved more deeply by profound music than by that which is trite.

It is your responsibility as the music specialist in the church to *identify* the effective music for your people and then produce it. But, in so doing, you must be very careful to maintain your credibility and influence. When the guitar first began its invasion of the sanctuary all church musicians were required to adopt an attitude toward it. Most musicians greeted it with a less than warm welcome, and understandably so. Many, by reacting violently to this "threat," and by letting their congregations know that they wanted nothing to do with this music, lost a large measure of their influence with many of their people.

In my own case, I made certain that the first person to play the guitar in the sanctuary of the church where I was director of music—that means *all* music—was the director of music. I did not play very much or very well, but by this simple act—which demonstrated only my willingness to experiment, not my wholehearted enthusiasm for this particular innovation—I maintained my influence over the uses which could be made of the guitar in our program. (We used it in fact only four more times that year in the Sunday morning service.) My opinions about the guitar were respected because I had tried it.

The very significant phenomenon which is symbolized by the guitar will be discussed in greater detail in a later chapter. It is mentioned here only to point out the critical nature of the musician's *public* reaction to a musical development of this type. You must maintain your credibility and your influence. The only way to do this is to prevent people from being able to predict accurately what your attitudes and feelings will be. If you do not remain open to new ideas and different kinds of music, your congregation will very quickly cease to listen to you; they will already know what you will say.

If we want to single out an adversary in this whole area, there is one far more deserving of attack than our high school youth, who are only trying to liberate our worship from its dullness, shallow piety, and hypocrisy. The young people should not be castigated for this. Our criticism should be leveled instead at those who are *exploiting* this "new church music" for profit. Separate the sometimes over-enthusiastic protest of our youth and their often remarkably rich music, and there is still a large residue (a good word here) of music left over which deserves to be quickly discarded by the church. This is the obviously contrived and highly commercial music that is no better than the contrived and commercial "gospel" music that so thoroughly tainted the otherwise worthy music of the early twentieth century, when evangelical Protestantism flourished in the tent.

One of the saddest chapters in the history of church music will be written about the "composers," "arrangers," "stars," record companies, sheet-music publishers, and agents who have struck it rich in the "sacred" music business. This business is nothing more than a popular music bonanza which extracts vast sums of money from an unsuspecting public who think they are buying a "spiritual blessing" but actually get no more than second-rate entertainment.

The job of the sincere church musician is to educate or cultivate in his congregation such a degree of sensitivity (that's a better word here than

... A Popular Music Bonanza ....

"appreciation") as will allow them to respond to a beauty in music that goes deeper than that which the jukebox can deliver.

Sacred music is not made sacred by the mere mention of God or Him or Savior, or some other replacement for the ordinary love-object of the popular song. Nor is it music that is so bland and dull as to avoid offending or disturbing anyone. Sacred music is music that is exciting, uplifting, moving—able to express and evoke emotions that can be touched in no other way.

Motivating the People to Learn

How does one go about "educating" his congregation in music? Till now I have made a conscious effort to keep this book from becoming a "how to" book. The effort will be interrupted at this point just long enough to provide some general comments on this important process.

First, as you contemplate the response or lack of response to your musical efforts, remember that people generally want to learn. They want to become more appreciative of quality in music. If you have not yet discovered this you have not even begun your task. Adult education programs in most communities are growing rapidly in all areas of learning. Concert-going is at an all-time high. Sales of records and tapes are booming. Music and learning are everywhere. The contemporary American churchman is the best-educated, most highly sophisticated listener the church has ever known. Our "students" are clearly willing and eager. It is up to us to be imaginative enough to devise ways to teach them.

Second, you must understand what learning involves. To be an effective teacher requires more of you than just the dissemination of information. It requires that you capture the congregation's interest and motivate them to learn. It requires a healthy *relationship* between teacher and learner which allows mutual understanding and free *two-way* communication to flourish. The relationship between one person and a group depends a great deal on the *image* of the leader. To be the leader in this type of effort you must have a good public image because, whether you are aware of it or not, you are a public personality. You have an image with your congregation, and it may or may not be the one you intend. You must give thought to this image and try to mold it so that people will respond to your program and have confidence in it even though they may not always understand it.

Music and Worship

Most of the music you furnish will be hymns and music for the services. The key to the layman's response to music in worship is his understanding not only of music, but of worship itself. You will almost always find that those who have strange ideas about music base their ideas on corresponding concepts of worship. If worship is a time to be harmlessly entertained, then the music should be tunefully entertaining. If worship is a time to be quiet, somber, and undisturbed, then the music will have to be quiet, somber, and undisturbing. If worship is a time to somehow get "back to God," to recapture feelings of the good old days when we were all more "religious," then the music will have to be the sentimental music of the past. Music's purpose is to enhance and reinforce the impact of worship for the worshiper. At best it can be only as effective as the worship itself.

When we begin to think of music as important only for itself in the church we soon forget that the responsibility for its use lies in great measure with those who determine the content and style of the worship in which that music will be used. This brings us to the minister. If the worship is poorly conceived and poorly planned, good music will not save it. If the minister leads the congregation to a healthy and creative approach to worship, poor music will be obviously inappropriate.

You must therefore crusade first and most strongly for better worship. You can do this as a musician without being accused of promoting your special interest. And to the degree that you and your minister succeed (together) you will be *asked by your people* to give them the best in music.

Music for Weddings

Another area of concern is music for weddings. Many musicians in the church find wedding music to be a problem. This is probably because of differences between the minister, the bride, and the musician in their understanding of music's place in the ceremony.

Begin your attack on this problem by discussing it with your minister. If you and he can come to an agreement about the wedding and the degree to which it should be considered an occasion of worship, he can then do a great deal to further your efforts. In his counseling and planning with the couple he can help them to understand what type of music should be used for their wedding.

Never fight, though, with brides or their mothers. Try to help them to choose wisely, but don't spoil their big day. As a part of the planning routine which is explained to them by the minister, or the secretary, or the wedding consultant, include the request that the bride sit down with you in your office to select the music well in advance of the big day. Talk with her about the details of her wedding, gain her confidence, and tell her she should choose music which fits her particular wedding, not necessarily what she has heard elsewhere. Keep suggesting good music and provide reasons for your suggestions that she can understand. Usually, the bride who listens will choose well.

You will be disappointed sometimes. You will fail sometimes. Brides and mothers of brides will insist on music that you would rather not play or sing. But, take the long view. Work with your minister and with each bride. Do your best. Keep records. You will discover that your efforts will pay off. Each year more and more brides will want better and better music.

Music for Funerals

Another problem area is music for funerals. All of us have been asked to play or sing some atrocious things at funerals. The simple matter of a very normal generation gap will find the favorite music of the deceased (who is usually very old) quite different from that favored by the musician (often quite young). Beyond that, ideas of what funerals are for have changed and are changing, and the conflict is made more intense.

There is really very little that the musician can do in this situation. At this time of bereavement widows and widowers are uneducable. Their only real contact with the world outside of the family is the minister. He can "improve" their funeral service as nobody else can.

It is my feeling, in this area as in many others, that the problem goes much deeper than the music. In view of current theological thinking, funeral practices as a whole are often so blatantly indefensible that the musician should not worry too much about the poor music he is asked to provide. This problem will have to be left to our clergy friends. The best we can do is to turn off the tremolo, play and sing good music when we are given the choice, and otherwise just grit our teeth and cooperate as requested.

Your responsibility to raise musical standards in *your* church does not give you license to destroy the relationship of persons with *their* church. The sacramental events which are marked by weddings and funerals are unforgettable moments for the church members involved. You must respect this and be patient and gentle with the person who experiences these events only once in his lifetime.

When every means of "education" has been tried, the most obvious and by far the best way to enrich your people's taste in music is simply to provide good music whenever possible and always do it well. Put your confidence in the variety of the great music of the church. It will communicate if given a chance. That is what makes it great. Give your people credit. They will respond more readily than you may think if you do your job well. Stop complaining and start practicing. Do your best and be enthusiastic. The responsibility for good music in the church is yours. When your people are not sensitive to good music, the blame is yours too.

Do You Go to Church?

It is ironic but sometimes true that the professional musician, who works long hours at the arduous tasks of making music and of organizing, leading, prodding, and cajoling other people to make music, sometimes actually enjoys *listening* to music less than an enthusiastic and responsive layman.

The vocation, which is essentially a pleasure-producing business, ceases to be also an avocation, and when the musician does have an opportunity for relaxation he gets as far away from music as he can.

In much the same way it is not unusual for the professional staff person in the church to be so involved in his daily organizational duties that he becomes more or less saturated with "church" and is in danger of becoming insensitive to the ministry, if not the message itself, of the gospel. The "producer," spending countless hours and vast amounts of energy striving to make the ministry of a church effective, can be so caught up in "dispensing" the program to the "consumers" that he has little opportunity to gain for himself the strength of spirit or food for living that he is helping to provide for others.

Personal Participation

In the service of worship, how can the musician participate as a member of the congregation when he is worrying about whether the altos will get lost in the contrapuntal section of the anthem, or whether B-flat on the *trompette* is going to stick when he hits it at the change of key, or whether Sara's voice will crack on her solo as it did in rehearsal? When the choir has to have a pitch for the response, what meaning does the prayer have for the organist? When the children pull each other's stoles from behind during the Scripture Reading (unless restrained by stern looks and shaking fingers) how can the director listen to the words being read? When every service of worship requires music of some kind, how can the musician himself ever worship?

And—the final irony—when we actually get a Sunday off and have the opportunity to attend a service without any responsibility, what do we do? We sit in the pew and say to ourselves during the entire service, "Why does she play the hymns that way?" or "There's a good idea; I'll have to remember that," or "That was awful; they shouldn't try that anthem with only two tenors."

The first and best answer to the problem of worship participation is to be prepared thoroughly before the service begins. If everyone (minister, musicians, readers) knows exactly what he is going to do and is confident that he can do it well, there will be a minimum of anxiety and distraction. Each leader can concentrate on the total service and be certain that when his turn comes he will be ready.

Beyond being prepared and confident, the devotional life of the church musician will have to be worked out by the individual in his own way. With determination, he will probably be able to solve the problem in one of two ways: either he will develop a "split-level" consciousness for worship so that he can think technically about the mechanics of what is happening and at the same time "tune in" as completely as possible to the content of the service itself, or he will have to find times apart from the regular worship of his church to fill this important need.

In terms of quantity alone the regularly employed musician is inevitably "exposed" to more worship than almost anyone else. He should at least try to gain as much as possible from this captive exposure.

Whatever form your own participation takes in worship, there is one significant attitude that can directly affect in great measure the benefit you will receive. This is your sense of involvement or identification, and it is not difficult to change if yours needs changing. When you think about the members of the congregation in your church do you think of them as "they" or "we"? When the minister is addressing the people in his sermon, for instance, do you say to yourself, "I wonder what *they* think of that?" Or, do you respond to his words yourself as a member of the congregation?

This question of the pronoun provides a very simple test. Try it on yourself. It may produce an accurate and revealing insight into your relationship with your church. If you are to participate in corporate worship you must feel that you are a part of the congregation. If you remove yourself from "them" and think of the worshipers as just an audience for "our" music, you will not be able to worship as a part of the worshiping community. You might just as well worship at home, since you have removed yourself from the "gathered people of God" and are only a mechanical aid to *their* worship. If, on the other hand, you find yourself responding to the parts of the service which do not require your leadership, you are probably allowing yourself to be one of the congregation and you have every opportunity of gaining almost as much as the worshiper in the pew.

It requires conscious discipline for any leader in worship to avoid becoming an objective observer who thinks of himself as above or at least removed from the laymen whom he leads in the service. What about you? The test is easy: Which personal pronoun begins your thoughts about your congregation? If you want to "go to church" yourself it had better be "we" and not "they."

Benefiting from Extra Involvements

Let us take this idea of attitude a step further, particularly as it applies to the full-time church musician. As you fulfill your many responsibilities outside of worship you will be required to attend meetings and programs of most of the groups in the church at one time or another. You will have to sing or play a hymn or accompany a singer or something. Occasionally you will even find yourself providing a musical item for a meeting without your having the faintest notion of why you are needed. Procrastinating program chairmen who have trouble shaping an effective program will turn desperately at the last minute to the "paid help" to get themselves out of a tight spot. And there you will be.

What is your attitude toward these duties? Do you resent them? Do you think of them as drudgery? Or can you gain something personally from attendance at a senior citizens tea or an auxiliary's installation of officers? I submit that, if you are open to the possibility, you can learn from and make good use of almost any experience. If you go expectantly, the least that will happen is the loss of your negative feelings about having to be somewhere you would rather not be.

Here are some possibilities for learning in what might appear to be unpromising situations. The reader can follow up with many more ideas like these.

The Fellowship Dinner

The fellowship dinner is a very important "ritual" that is a part of the program of most churches. There are sound theological and even biblical reasons why congregations feel they must "commune" together around the dinner table. All-church dinners will happen two or three times a year at least, and the musician is usually called upon to provide a portion of the program.

Do you realize how important these events can be to you? If you skip the meal itself, come just for your part of the program, and then leave, you are missing a golden opportunity in several ways.

Contrary to what it may seem, the main purpose of a church dinner has nothing to do with either the food or the program. What really matters, as any intelligent minister will tell you, is what happens in the conversations before, during, and after. I have seen a skillful minister make the equivalent of thirty to forty pastoral calls at one church dinner. You can do the same. Here is your chance to get acquainted, cultivate friends, recruit choir members, and demonstrate your concern for people who need it. If there is a ten-minute period of confusion while dishes are cleared, get up and circulate among the crowd. Not only will you be more visible to your people, you will gain their confidence because you are one of them.

Youth Activities

Attend as many youth activities as you can. To work well with a youth choir you must know them and understand them as much as possible. If you can be with them when they are having fun, or working, or learning, you can discover more easily what their needs are and what you can expect from them. Youth have a great deal to offer if you will open yourself to them. Their effervescence and enthusiasm can pick you up like a tonic if you will allow yourself to be a part of their group.

Ladies' Groups

The women's organizations are among the most important in the church. Like it or not, a great deal of the health and well-being of a congregation depends upon the women. You will need their help for your program in many ways. You can always use their support. Be cooperative, enthusiastic, and willing to help with your talent and they will find many ways to repay you.

There are always two or three (and often more) genuine "saints" among the women of a church, usually persons eighty or ninety years of age but young in spirit, who will be a pleasure to get to know. Often these women can be "ministers" to you, and you will be inspired and uplifted just from spending time with them.

Business Meetings

Many musicians avoid the business meetings of a church at every opportunity. Dull, routine, interminable meetings seem to be a waste of time—except when you are leading a dull, routine, interminable meeting yourself. There are things to be gained, however, from attending as many meetings as your schedule will allow.

First of all, if you understand and are a part of the committees and boards of the church you will learn quickly how best to get action on policies and projects that you yourself propose. When a committee is thought of as "we" rather than "they" your chances of favorable action are infinitely greater.

You also have the opportunity in a business meeting to observe and learn the skills of leadership. Watch how meetings progress or stagnate. Figure out why. Try to discover what makes a good or a bad leader of the group. Absorb all you can about the dynamics of group action and morale. As a choir director you are the leader of a group and you need to know as much as you can about organization and leadership. The best training in effective leadership of a group is to watch a leader who is effective. The next best is to watch one who isn't.

All of this may seem to be above and beyond the call of duty for the musician, and in fact it is. But there are definite benefits to be gained from doing whatever you can in these ways. You can gain personally from your relationship with the people, and, whether you like to admit it or not, some of the finest people around are in churches. Your people will respect you and listen to you and they will support you and your program more consistently if you are a visible part of the congregation. And finally, you will coordinate and cooperate better with the total church program if you know what that program is. When you work for the church you have two possibilities: you can be a paid technician who does only what he is told and never oversteps the limits of his job analysis—and you may survive. Or, you can do what you expect laymen to do and "go to church" yourself—to your benefit and that of the church as well.

Church Musicians Should Be People

In this chapter we will try to summarize what has been said and arrive at an overall concept of the task of the church musician. We will then attempt to exorcise ourselves by the healthy process of confession as we painfully point out what a church musician should *not* be. All of this will clear our minds and our consciences for what remains in the final chapter—a blind look into the future, where this writer's opinion of what lies ahead is probably as good as that of anyone who reads this book.

I must now fulfill an earlier promise and try to lay to rest any lingering feelings that to scrutinize closely one's relationship to people in the church, to try to understand what makes that relationship successful, and to discover what efforts are required to get people to respond in certain ways is more a study in politics than in religion. Indeed, the effective worker in the church must be a psychologist, a salesmen, yes, even a politician in the best sense of those terms. It is absolutely vital to your work that you understand how and why people behave as they do. It makes sense, too, to attempt what is necessary in order to help people respond to the good news of the gospel in the best way.

Perhaps the only thing that needs to be questioned is our motives, and these are above reproach if we keep our eyes fixed on the proper goal. Most simply stated our goal should be: music for the effective worship of our people, not worship as a convenient vehicle for our music.

The Task of the Church Musician

We may start by saying that a church musician should be a churchman first and a musician second. At this point we usually hide behind that pious phrase about "Christian character" without feeling the necessity to spell out what it really means. If we were to describe Christian character in the ideal church musician, we would have to say that his first concern is always for *persons* rather than for ideas, ideals, or even music itself. No other explanation of the phrase is either necessary or adequate.

Therefore, the church musician cannot afford the luxury of behaving like a concert artist who puts the performance of music above all other considerations. In the church our "artistic" temperament, our personal feelings, even our musical opinions will sometimes have to be pushed to the background as we think of the greater task of ministering to persons.

The real job of the musician is threefold, involving worship, education, and music—and this sequence probably represents a good order of value for these three areas of the church program. People gather first to worship. For the past twenty years at least, not many people have been concerned about worship. Those who have, have usually been musicians. The greatest weakness in the seminary training and organizational structures of the major denominations is the appalling lack of emphasis on worship.

Many musicians have carried the "cause" for better and more effective worship almost singlehandedly in the local church. Now, when the drive for "worship renewal" is forcing every church to reexamine its patterns, there are far too few clergymen or laymen who have studied worship seriously enough over the years to know what they are doing.

As musicians we must continue to press for integrity, vitality, and effectiveness in worship. We must be very careful that we are not just reactionaries when it comes to experimentation in worship. We must join in and lead the "cause." No other task is more important to the church.

The second most important area of the church musician's interest is education. We must all be educated to worship, to love, to give, and to mobilize for mission in the world. For this writer, education at all levels, and especially *adult* Christian education is the greatest hope for the future.

And third, yes third, music is our job. Music is a *tool*, a powerful tool which can be integral and critical in both worship and education. Our job is to sharpen this tool and show people how to use it to make their Christian experience more meaningful.

What Kind of a Person Are You?

It is now time for us to turn and look at ourselves in the light of these ideas and see what kind of *persons* we are, regardless of how well we play or sing or direct choirs. By way of helping you with your "confession"—and me with mine—we turn again to the rather questionable technique of drawing word pictures of one-dimensional people to illustrate a point. Again, all of these will be negative examples. The faults depicted will be found in most of us, though hardly to the extent here portrayed. Interestingly enough, each of these characteristics really represents virtue carried to extreme. Do you recognize yourself in any of these people?

Busy Technician

"I'm paid to do the music in the church and that is all. I'm too busy with my regular job to do any *more*." He does what he is asked to do. His music may or may not be appropriate, he doesn't give too much thought to that. He may or may not be very conscientious in his work.

Twenty years ago this may have been enough. In the future it will not. He misses the point that it isn't necessary that he do *more* or give more *time*. What is important is his *attitude* and his *manner* of working. He must be a *church* musician even if for only two hours a week.

74

The Big Ego

"Music comes first for me and should for everybody else in *my* program." This musician jealously guards the people in his choirs and frowns on their participation anywhere else in the church's program. He fights schedule battles continually with everybody who comes near one of his dates. He judges every policy and expenditure of the church on the basis of what is in it for music.

This stance for the church musician is unrealistic, untheological, unnecessary, and self-defeating. If he is always fighting, people will fight back. If he doesn't cooperate, people will not cooperate with him. He must put himself and his music in the proper perspective and realize that there are other things more important than music.

Erudite, Artistic Snob

"Only the best music has any value at all. I am the musician so I know what is best." This musician is judgmental, self-righteous, and impossible to work beside. His most serious problem is that he usually equates an individual's level of sophistication and understanding of music with his worth as a person. If someone does not measure up musically, he doesn't measure up—period.

A concern for great music has a strong place in the church. When that concern steps on people, its place is gone.

Bandwagon Jumper

"It's poor music and even worse theology, but the people like it, so I use it." This person is most concerned about what the people like. He will do anything that seems to be popular. He looks to other musicians for his ideas and judges them by their immediate response. In these days of uncertainty he may even rationalize that he must do the popular thing to protect his job.

His problem is that his work lacks integrity. It is not based on strong feelings or convictions. This musician must remember his responsibility to teach, to help people grow. He must think enough of his ideas to assert himself.

Denomination-Hopper

"I can provide music for any denomination. After all, music is ecumenical." He will attempt to "ply his trade" anywhere that he can get a good

position. Too often he gets caught in a church or a denomination that does not match his personal expression of faith or, more important, his level of interest or type of training in liturgical matters. Denomination-hopping is a practice which is more or less peculiar to musicians. It is also one which ought to be discouraged (at least, that is my own conviction).

Victorian Conservative

"If only we could get back to the glorious music of *my* youth." The answer to that is simple: we can never go back.

Sour Martyr

"We musicians are being persecuted. No one cares about good music anymore. Our program is ignored." This musician's stance deserves no sympathy either. His program probably has earned the indifference it receives.

Desperate Escapee

"I've got to change fields. There is no future in church music and that job over there sure looks good." Fascinated by the handwriting on the economic wall, he is studying accounting at night school, or selling real estate on his day off, or dreaming of the day when he can get into that other field that looks so much easier and so much more lucrative than church music.

There is some of this in all of us. It takes courage to stay in the church today. But we must not give up. Even though the church may change, it is not going to die. There is hope for us, but only if we learn our *nonmusical* lessons well. Our survival depends partly on our opening ourselves to change.

We will summarize by saying that our task is to help strengthen the church in its worship and in its education *through* the use of our music. We must be concerned about the whole church, but not to the point of demanding that its leadership conform to our ideas of what it should be. We should know the limits of our influence and our responsibility, but not let our concern be limited.

We must work hard to do the very best we can so that what we do will be important. But we must be open to the possibility that some of our efforts might not be needed anymore. If we can be truly church musicians and not just musicians in the church, there will always be an important place for us to serve.

SHOULD I LEARN to PLAY the Guitar?

The surge of interest in music—folk music, pop music, rock music—performed by what are essentially nonmusicians in the church is one of the most important developments in church music in many years. It has happened not only independently of any real help from the church musician himself, but in most respects *in spite of* indifference or outright opposition from those of us who are responsible for the musical life of the church. The force of this spontaneous and almost universal phenomenon should say at least two things to us very clearly.

First, it is obvious that the message that we musicians have always thought was ours to proclaim is now coming back to us more clearly and more insistently than we could ever say it ourselves: *music is important in the church.* Without entering the various debates about the worth of the new kinds of music being used in worship we can safely observe that our laymen, and especially our young laymen, are telling us they need music to help them give expression to their faith. Music *is* important.

Second, it is clear that in spite of our hard work and deep concern over the years, we have failed. It is disappointing that the clamor is for a kind of music that is quite different from the "good" music we have been trying to "sell" all these years. To have the initiative for music-making in the church seized from us so quickly, enthusiastically, and thoroughly, by kids who can neither sing nor play their guitars very well and by "song writers" who have found a market that is more lucrative and less competitive than they should have expected, is certainly an event that is without precedent in the history of church music. When you look at the arms and ammunition we have assembled (measured in MSM's and SMD's,), the experience and the man-hours in the practice room, it is incredible that we have lost our positions of leadership almost before we realized that we were being challenged. And our failure is this: with all of our training and effort and skill we have not yet come up with a contemporary musical idiom that is simple enough for the nonmusician to use in worship and at the same time strong enough to inspire and move people, and to constitute an abiding contribution to the worship of coming generations.

The Demands of the Future

As we work through this failure, and hopefully correct it, the future is going to make some demands upon us. Many of these demands will have little to do with music itself.

First, the future will demand that musicians put their primary concern on the church and its people rather than simply on the music. Music is simply our tool, our means to express and to live out that primary concern. The implications of this priority will touch many aspects of our work. It may affect our attitude toward choir attendance in a day when families are being pulled apart from all sides and an occasional weekend away from home may be the only means of retaining any family life at all. It may affect our choices of music in a day when a congregation includes people of ever more varied backgrounds.

It is possible to carry on a strong music program in a complex and fast-paced society, but it is difficult. People more and more are guarding carefully what sociologists call their "discretionary time," time in which they can themselves choose what to do. They will put their time and their commitment only where they feel it will be more worthwhile than a number of other choices that they have. The musician will have to make every minute count that he asks of the busy laymen in his choirs.

Second, we will have to broaden our understanding of the uses which can be made of the music we provide. "Formal" and "informal" are rather inadequate terms for describing worship. It is possible, however, that there may soon develop two different kinds of worship using quite different kinds of music. Festival days and celebrations of important seasons of the church year may employ the strong, immortal music of the ages and the exciting and complex contemporary music of the serious composer. For this, no guitar will ever serve. No amount of amplification will enable it to lead large numbers of people in singing; it does not carry a clear melody line. The organ is the only large instrument that can do this well and still be controlled by one performer.

But the same church may also have smaller, more frequent worship experiences in which the emphasis is on a feeling of community, on individual expression. In these services much of the music will be written and produced (perhaps with guitars) by laymen themselves.

Whatever direction worship moves in the future, it is unrealistic to expect that there will be only one form using only one type of music—least of all the type that any one of us personally prefers. We must expect and even encourage the use of many kinds of music—and the experimentation with various kinds of worship—until some general patterns emerge. To oppose this inevitable search, to cling inflexibly to an idea of worship from the past will simply result in the decline of our influence in the continuing search.

The third demand which we must meet will be a call upon the musician to work in other areas of the church's program besides music. Various "prophets" today are predicting many different forms for the future church, but those who see the local church surviving agree that its program will become more and more complex. It follows directly that the job of the musician will also become more complex.

Doubtless we will need to move, for example, in the direction of the other arts. Probably the musician will be asked to coordinate a program which will include art, drama, dance, and literature. This will not signify any downgrading of the importance of music but simply an increase in the complexity of the church's total program. If we want to be a part of that program, our share will have to increase with it.

The Promise of Openness

Through all of this we must remain open to change. Change is going to continue and will probably accelerate. Much of a person's success during periods of change depends on his attitude toward change itself. Certain things that are basic will surely remain in the life of the church, but we will have to expect and allow for a variety of styles and instruments and people to join us in the making of music. The only way to maintain a position of leadership in this change is to join in and lead.

We are hearing from all sides, including the jukebox, that music is important to the faith. It is clear that we have not yet found the type of music that will unite our congregations (and our musicians). It may be that no single musical style will ever again be able to do this, but we must try.

We must be positive and optimistic about the future. There is really a great deal of evidence to suggest that the future for the musician in our

... the CHAOS that is
CHURCH MUSIC today

society is a hopeful one. In the nonverbal, postliterate world of Marshall McLuhan, when the written and spoken word are becoming obsolete, the only means left to man for expressing his praise will be music and the arts. When ecological crusaders finally get us to clean up our environment and to value the quality of life rather than merely its quantity, we shall surely turn and attack also the pollution of sound that follows us everywhere from the electronic speaker. And, when current theologians are finally heard and understood, all of us in the church will be seeking to feel and to express a depth of emotion that only music and the arts can touch.

The challenge for the trained musician has been sounded by the sixteen-year-old monotone who dropped out of the children's choir in the sixth grade, but is now the lead "singer" in his "group." Can we serve the church of the 70's by bringing some order out of the chaos that is church music today?

The future of music in the church *is* threatening to the one-dimensional "artistic" personality who wants to be paid by a congregation for producing his weekly concert. But it is wide open and inviting for the musician *who is also a person* concerned about others and about the church and its ministry to a troubled world.